Fun Thanksgiving Jokes and Riddles for Kids and Family

300 Funny Turkey Stuffing Jokes
&
300 Fun Gobble Gobble Riddles & Trick Questions
That Kids and Family Will Enjoy

Riddleland

Tables of Content

The Try Not to Laugh Challenge Jokes Thanksgiving Turkey Stuffing Edition

Fun Thanksgiving Riddles & Trick Questions For Kids and Family – Gobble Gobble Edition

The
Try Not To
Laugh Challenge
Joke Book

Thanksgiving Edition

300 Funny Turkey Stuffing Jokes

That Kids and Family Will Enjoy

With Fun Illustrations

Riddleland

Check out some of the fun illustrations that comes with the jokes

More fun illustrations

Introduction

"Not what we say about our blessings, but how we use them is the true measure of our Thanksgiving"~W.T. Purkiser

We would like to personally thank you for purchasing this book. **The Try Not to Laugh Challenge Joke Book: Thanksgiving Edition** is different from other joke books. It is not meant to be read alone, but instead it is a game to be played with siblings, friends, family or between two people that would like to prove who is a better comedian. Time to see who has the funny bone in the family!

These jokes are written to be fun and easy to read. Children learn best when they are playing. Reading can help increase that vocabulary and comprehension. They have also many other benefits such as:

- **Bonding** – It is an excellent way for parents and their children to spend some quality time and create some fun and memorable memories.

- **Confidence Building** – When parents give the riddles, it creates a safe environment for children to burst out answers even if they are incorrect. This helps the children to develop self confidence in expressing themselves.

- **Improve Vocabulary** – Jokes are usually written in easy to advance words, therefore children will need to understand these words before they can share the jokes.

- **Better reading comprehension** – Many children can read at a young age but may not understand the context of the sentences. Riddles can help develop the children's interest to comprehend the context before they can share it to their friends.

- **Sense of humor** –Funny creative jokes can help children develop their sense of humor while getting their brains working.

Rules of the Game!

The Goal is to make your opponent laugh

- Face your opponent.
- Stare at them!
- Make funny faces and noises to throw your opponent off
- Take turns reading the jokes out loud to each other
- When someone laughs, the other person wins a point

First person to get 5 points, is crowned The Champion!

Alert: Bonus Book for the Kids!

https://bit.ly/riddlelandbonusbook

Thank you for buying this book, We would like to share a special bonus as a token of appreciation. It is collection 50 original jokes, riddles and 2 funny stories

Chapter 1: Turkey Stuffing Challenge

"Let us be grateful to the people who make us happy. They are the charming gardeners who make our souls blossom." ~ Marcel Proust

1) If a large turkey is called a gobbler, what is a small one called?

Goblet

2) How do small turkeys respond when they are being bullied by the larger ones?

They say "peck on someone your own size!

3) What do you call a turkey that likes stealing wallets?

A robber gobbler!

4) What is a Turkey's favorite fantasy movie?

Turkey on the Potter and the Gobblet of Fire

5) How did the first cows travel to America?

They sailed on the moo-flower!

6) What do pilgrims call their friends?

Pal-grims!

7) Why did the turkey blush?

It was looking at the salad dressing.

8) What Thanksgiving superhero has wings and a sidekick?

Beak-man and Robin!

9) What's the first thing turkeys check on TV?

The feather forecast!

10) Why didn't the cook season the Thanksgiving turkey?

Because he had no thyme!!

11) What is a turkey's favorite supervillain?

The green gobble-in!

12) What is a turkey's favorite apparatus for science experiments?

Beak-ers!

13) How did the Puritans discover America?

Pure-ly by chance!

14) What special occasion do the dad turkeys get gifts from their children?

Feather's day!

15) If the pilgrims sailed on the Mayflower, what do students sail on?

Scholar-ships!

16) Why did the turkey go to the theme park?

To ride on the roller-roaster!

17) What vegetable do policemen eat on Thanksgiving?

Corn on the cop!

18) Who is baby corn's dad?

Pop-corn!

19) What did the guests say when leaving the Thanksgiving dinner?

Good-pie everybody!

20) What do you call lots of gravy on a boat?

Wavy gravy!

21) What is the best chart you can use to visualize your Thanksgiving dinner?

Pumpkin pie chart!

22) What do you call a turkey telling sarcastic jokes?

A smirky turkey!

23) What do you call a turkey waddling through the mud?

A murky turkey!

24) What do you call a Thanksgiving feast with hotdogs?

A Franks-giving feast!

25) What do you call a turkey who drinks a lot of coffee!

A perky turkey! Street

26) What does creamed corn taste like?

Taste pretty a-maize-ing!

27) What do sailors serve their turkey with?

Navy gravy!

28) How does a limping turkey behave?

It goes "Wobble, wobble, wobble!"

29) What do you call a cow with no more legs?

Ground beef!

30) What is Dracula's second favorite holiday to Halloween?

Fangs-giving!

31) What do bankers do every November?

Celebrate banks-giving!

32) What happens if you eat too much corn on Thanksgiving?

You get an "ear" ache!

33) Why do scarecrows normally have trouble finding the cornfield?

Because they usually get corn-fused!

34) What language do pilgrims need to learn before they graduate?

Pilgrammar

35) What is a robot turkey powered by?

A potato chip!

36) What do grumpy people celebrate in November?

Cranks-giving!

37) How do pumpkins describe the autumn scenery?

By saying how gourd-geous it is!

38) What do you call a Thanksgiving dinner that has lots of bread?

A yeast feast!

39) What kind of test do sweet potatoes excel in?

A yam exam!

40) What are the sleepiest things on a Thanksgiving table?

The nap-kins!

41) What do you call a turkey stuffing that is out of breath?

A puffing stuffing!

42) What did the turkey to the bread in the oven?

You're toast!

43) What do you call a really smart turkey?

A geek beak!

44) What do you call a message sent to a sweet potato?

A yam-gram!

45) What kind of jelly do potatoes like most?

Yam jam!

46) What is a vegetable garden's favorite type of music?

Brocc n' Roll!

47) How did the pancake feel when the cornbread gave it a compliment?

The pancake felt flattered!

48) How does a Turkey spend time on the Internet?

It Google, Google, Googles!

49) What does a selfish person call Thanksgiving?

Thanks-taking!

50) What do you call a strange turkey?

A quirky turkey!

51) What makes a muffin similar to a baseball team?

Both of them depend on the batter!

52) How do you give a punch to people on Thanksgiving without hurting them?

By mixing pineapple juice, lemonade, orange juice and cranberry juice and serving it to them!

53) Why is cranberry juice needed on Thanksgiving?

To ensure everyone has a fruitful holiday!

54) Why did scarecrow skip school yesterday?

Because the scarecrow had hay fever!

55) What do you call the leader of a group of corn?

The kernel!

56) Who is in charge of saying the Thanksgiving prayer?

The feast priest!

57) What do math teachers do at a Thanksgiving feast before eating?

They count their blessings!

58) Why wasn't the turkey stuffing happy with its job?

Because it wanted a higher celery!

59) Why happens when two turkeys argue about something petty?

They squabble, squabble, squabble!

60) What is a cat's favorite Thanksgiving side dish?

Mashed purr-tatoes!

61) What did the turkey from a galaxy far far away say?

May the fork be with you!

62) Why do some scarecrows like lifting weights?

So they can get strawnger

63) What do skunks celebrate on November?

Stanksgiving!

64) What was the pumpkin recalling after sharing stories of previous Thanksgiving feasts?

The gourd old days!

65) What do you call a turkey that goes meow?

A purr-key!

66) If a bunny has a knee, what does a turkey have?

A key!

67) What do you call a cranberry's mother's mother?

A cranmother!

68) When does the Thanksgiving bread roll rise?

When you yeast expect it!

69) Why do people roast turkeys on Thanksgiving Day?

Because Thanksgiving never falls under a fry-day!

-

70) What is a turkey's favorite Thanksgiving song?

God save the kin!

71) Why is the hardworking family so stressed at the Thanksgiving table?

Because they had a lot on their plates!

72) What did the pumpkin pie tell the boy who wanted to eat the pecan pie?

The trip is too long to walk!

73) What happens when you make a cranberry sad?

It becomes a blueberry.

74) What is Frankenstein's favorite Thanksgiving dinner?

Monster mash-ed potatoes with lots of grave-y!

75) What do you call a snake with no clothes?

You are nuts!

76) What do you call a pumpkin who ensures the safety of swimmers?

A life-gourd!

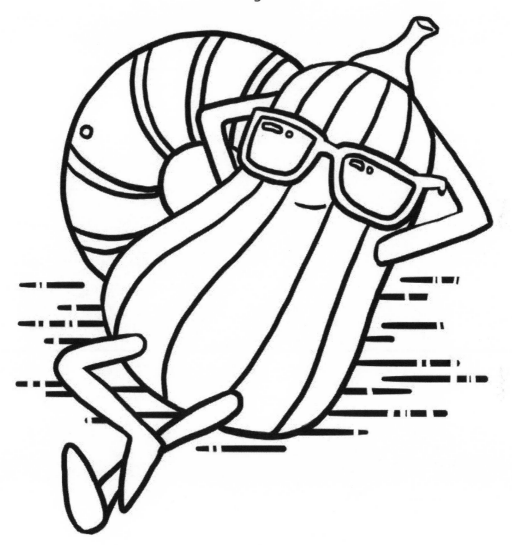

77) Why did the turkey cross the road back and forth?

To prove he wasn't chicken!

78) Why do pilgrims' pants keep falling down?

Because their buckles are on their hats!

79) What is a pilgrim's favorite snack?

A pil-graham cracker!

80) Why did the sweet potato decide to join a band?

So the entire band can have a yam session!

81) What is a turkey's favorite pie?

A tur-key lime pie!

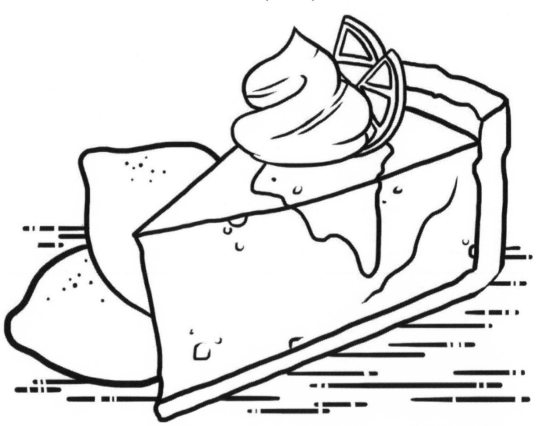

82) What is the most expensive Thanksgiving food served in a luxury hotel?

Suite potatoes!

Chapter 2 Gobble Gobble Q&A Challenge

"Give thanks for unknown blessings already on their way." ~ Native American Saying

1) Where's the best place to find pilgrims nowadays?

In history books!

2) Why was the pumpkin sad?

It was going through a pretty rough patch.

3) What is the difference between Turkey and chicken?

One is a country and the other is a poultry.

4) What does a pilgrim usually dress up as on Halloween?

The pil-grim reaper!

5) Why do pilgrims avoid telling secrets in cornfields?

Because the corn have ears!

6) What do you get when a turkey lays an egg on a slope?

You get an eggroll!

7) How did the Mayflower show its love for America?

By hugging its shore!

8) What do call a turkey running away?

Fast food!

9) What do turkeys, chickens and ducks all have in common?

They are all fowl animals!

10) What do you call a farming vehicle that is very good at finding the right angle?

A pro-tractor!

11) Why do bananas need to use sunscreen?

Because they brown and peel easily

12) When turkeys get arrested, what is the common crime committed?

Fowl play!

13) What does The Hulk say when somebody attempts to steal his Thanksgiving mashed potatoes?

Hulk mashed!

14) When do the pilgrims say "God bless America"?

Whenever they hear America sneeze!

15) What dessert do turkeys love most?

Homemade peach gobbler!

16) What is the difference between a pirate and a cranberry farmer?

Pirates bury their treasure while cranberry farmers treasure their berries.

17) What time is it when an elephant sits on a fence?

It's time to fix the fence!

18) Why are apple pies popular in Thanksgiving dinners?

Because they look pretty a-peeling!

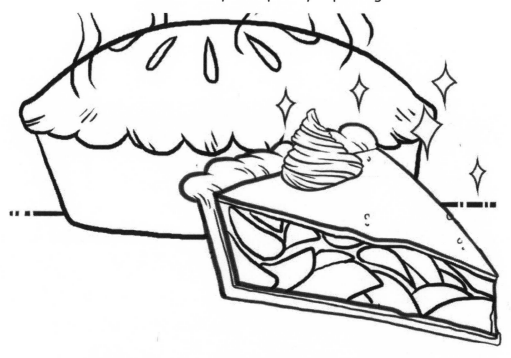

19) What do you call a snake with no clothes?

You are nuts!

20) What happens when Winter comes?

Autumn leaves!

21) Why did the farmer move the modem into the barn?

So he can have stable Wi-Fi!

22) Why do the cows love to hide up in the mountains in November?

Because the steaks have never been higher on Thanksgiving season!

23) What is everybody's favorite spice on Thanksgiving Day?

Pumpkin spice!

24) What is the top thing kids should be thankful about on Thanksgiving?

They should be thankful they aren't turkeys!

25) What is a turkey's favorite ball sport?

Squash!

26) What is a turkey's favorite children's novel?

The Wonderful Gizzard of Oz!

27) What is the one thing that a turkey needs to see the fairy godmother?

A wishbone!

28) Why are turkeys so bad at baseball?

Because they keep hitting fowl balls!

29) How did the turkey lose the boxing match?

The turkey got the stuffing knocked out of him!

30) What happens when you mix a turkey with an octopus?

You get enough drumsticks for the whole family!

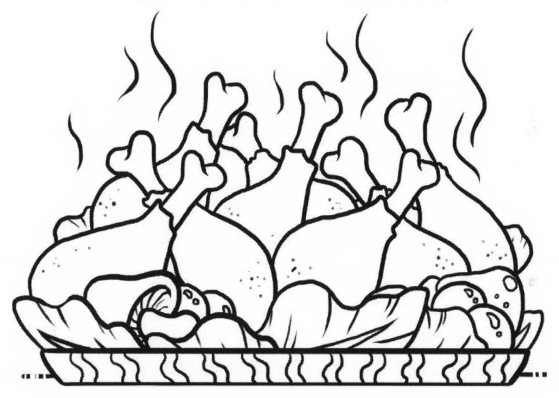

31) What did the general do for his army on Thanksgiving?

He gave tanks to them!

32) Why did the turkey have school detention?

The turkey was caught using fowl language!

33) What's the weather like when it is raining turkeys?

Pretty fowl weather!

34) When did the pilgrims decide to buy the Mayflower?

They waited for it to go on sail!

35) Why do turkeys lay their eggs?

Because if they dropped their eggs, the eggs would break!

36) What do comedians refer to Thanksgiving as?

Pranks-giving!

37) Why did the grandfather ask his grandson to put on a winter coat?

Because he was told grandma is cooking up a storm!

38) What is the best time of the evening to have Thanksgiving dinner?

During half-time!

39) What do turkeys use to draw Thanksgiving dinners?

Crayon-berries!

40) What is a sweet potato's favorite children's book?

Green Eggs and Yam!

41) Why did the turkeys ask the Grinch for help?

Because they wanted the Grinch to steal Thanksgiving!

42) What modern job would best fit a pilgrim if they were around today?

Computer pilgramming!

43) What makes a Thanksgiving turkey so expensive?

When it has 24 carrots!

44) Why isn't the scarecrow very good at telling funny jokes?

Because the jokes were too corn-y!

45) Why do people often get smart on Thanksgiving season?

Because Thanksgiving is held on Know-vember!

46) What do you call a pie that is too scared to be on the Thanksgiving dinner table?

A shy pie!

47) Why wasn't the cranberry present at the Thanksgiving feast?

Because it got bogged down at work!

48) What kind of games do Thanksgiving desserts enjoy playing?

I spy with my little pie!

49) Why do all the different Thanksgiving pies get along well?

Because they see each other pie to pie!

50) Why didn't the pilgrim feel like baking bread?

Because it's a pretty crummy job!

51) What happened after the corn tried to fight the spinach?

Both of them got creamed!

52) Where do mice normally park their boats?

At the Hickory Dickory Dock!

53) Where do you find a turkey with no legs?

Exactly where you left it!

54) Why do turkeys do nothing but gobble?

Because nobody ever taught them any good table manners!

55) Why do potatoes serve as great detectives?

Because they always keep their eyes peeled!

56) What's the best way to show good manners after finishing your Thanksgiving meal?

By saying "I'm so thank-full!"

57) Why did the turkey spend hours getting ready for the Thanksgiving party?

Because she heard the other turkeys in attendance will be well-dressed!

58) What is the difference a turkey and a chicken?

Only the chicken celebrates Thanksgiving!

59) What is the cutest season of the year?

Awwww-tumn

60) What's blue and covered in feathers?

A turkey holding its breath!

61) What area on the Mayflower do the pilgrims play cards?

On the deck!

62) What food gets along with all the other Thanksgiving dishes?

Sweet potatoes!

63) Why did the roasted turkey refuse to cross the road?

Because it didn't have the guts to do it!

64) What kind of dog is paired best with cream cheese?

A beagle!

65) What fruit do scarecrows like the most?

Straw-berries!

66) What do you call a really fat pumpkin?

A plump-kin!

67) Why did the turkeys decide to dress up in silly outfits for Thanksgiving?

So others will think that the turkeys have bad taste!

68) What do you call a turkey chained to a monkey and a donkey?

A keychain!

69) How do you make a sausage roll?

By pushing it down a hill!

70) What sound does a turkey's smartphone makes when there is an incoming call?

It goes wing, wing!

71) What is a Thanksgiving pumpkin's favorite superhero movie?

Gourd-ians of the Galaxy!

72) Why did the turkey invite the other turkeys to his place during the summer?

Because the turkey was hosting a pool-try party!

73) What do Thanksgiving and Halloween have in common?

Halloween has goblins and Thanksgiving has gobblers!

74) Why are carpenters very good at serving your Thanksgiving dinner?

Because they know how to properly carve a turkey!

75) What do you get when you mix two different songs about potatoes?

A mash-up!

76) What is the secret key to a great Thanksgiving dinner?

A tur-key!

77) What three steps do you do when you see a Thanksgiving fire?

Stop, drop, and pass the rolls!

78) How do Turkeys act on a space station?

They go Hubble, Hubble, Hubble!

79) Why did the cook decide to spill his soup?

Because there was a leek in the pot!

80) What do you call a poultry that is good in algebra?

A mathema-chicken!

81) What do you call a chicken-proof lawn?

Impeck-able!

82) What comes out after a turkey picks its nose?

A gooble goober!

83) How long does it normally take to make butter?

It takes an e-churn-ity!

84) What is the best thing to put in a pumpkin pie?

Your teeth of course!

85) Why did the pilgrim suddenly start feeling ticklish after he ate the turkey?

Because he forgot to pluck the turkey's feathers.

86) What would pilgrims be most famous for if they are still alive today?

Their age!

87) How do you fix a broken slice of pizza?

Just add tomato paste!

88) What are cranberries most afraid of?

BOO-berries!

89) What is the best song to sing while the turkey is cooking?

It's all about the baste!

90) How do scarecrows greet their siblings?

Hay brothers and sisters!

91) What happens when it rains potatoes over a street?

They make spuddles

92) Why are sweet potatoes capable of getting lots of work done?

Because they are not couch potatoes!

93) What do you call a single, lonely ear of corn?

A uni-corn!

94) What would you get if Thanksgiving was to be celebrated on April?

Feaster Sunday!

95) Why are turkeys considered the fastest eaters?

Because they always practice gobbling!

96) What do you get when you mix a pumpkin with Bigfoot?

A sas-squash!

97) What did the fox say to the stuffed turkey?

Pleased to eat you!

98) What did papa pumpkin say when he dropped baby pumpkin?

Oh my gourd!

99) What do you call a lobster that is afraid of very tight spaces?

Claw-strophobic!

100) What did the gravy say before it got poured on the mashed potatoes?

I got you covered!

101) What is the most dangerous pie?

A pie-thon!

102) Which side of the turkey has the most feathers?

The out-side!

103) What kind of crawling insect likes apple juice?

A cider spider!

104) What do you call a chicken that can do magic tricks?

A ma-chicken!

105) Why are fish so easy to weigh?

Because fish have their own scales!

106) What do you call a person who looks after chickens?

A chicken tender!

107) What do teddy bears and Thanksgiving turkeys have in common?

Both are full of stuffing!

108) What is the result when you divide the circumference of a pumpkin by its diameter?

Pumpkin pi.

109) Why was the dog trying to chase the band in the Thanksgiving parade?

The dog wanted to bury the trombones!

110) What do you use to send turkeys through postal mail?

Bird class mail!

111) Where do the toughest turkeys come from?

Hard-boiled eggs!

112) Why did the hunter skip on turkey last Thanksgiving?

Because he went on a wild goose chase!

113) Why did the turkey retire from baseball?

Because he couldn't make it to first baste!

114) Who helps the smaller pumpkins cross the street?

The crossing gourd!

115) What do pampered cows produce?

Spoiled milk!

116) Why is Humpty Dumpty's favorite season autumn?

Because he always had great falls!

117) If an orange comes from an orange tree, where does a turkey come from?

A poul-tree!

118) Why was the baker not so excited after preparing a garlic pumpkin pie?

Because he had mixed fillings about it!

119) What kind of turkey would you serve if Thanksgiving and April Fools were on the same day?

Tofu turkey!

120) What do pampered cows produce?

Spoiled milk!

121) Why is Humpty Dumpty's favorite season autumn?

Because he always had great falls!

122) If an orange comes from an orange tree, where does a turkey come from?

A poul-tree!

123) How come Albert Einstein never celebrated Thanksgiving?

Because he was too busy celebrating Thinksgiving!

124) Where did the pilgrims stand after they landed?

On their feet!

125) When is the appropriate time for a turkey to take off its Halloween costume?

On the day after Thanksgiving!

126) What do autumn trees say when they like each other?

They say "I'm falling for you!"

127) What do trees tell other trees when they need some peace and quiet?

They say "Leaf me alone!"

128) What do you get when you cross a turkey and a droid?

R2-Beak2!

129) What did the turkey in the sauna say?

What is that lovely smell?

130) How do scarecrows drink their cranberry juice?

Using a straw!

131) When is the best time for a turkey to sneak out of the oven?

When the roast is clear!

132) What is the only musical part of a turkey?

The drumsticks!

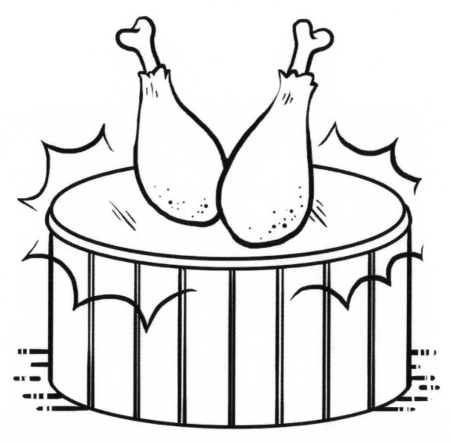

133) What do you call celebrating Thanksgiving with folks other than your parents?

Friendsgiving!

134) What do you call a turkey who is awful at bowling?

A gutter-ball turkey!

135) What's the best dance to perform on Thanksgiving Day?

The turkey trot!

136) Why should you avoid setting the turkey near the dessert?

Because the turkey will gobble, gobble, gobble it up!

137) Why is the scarecrow all alone in the cornfield while the others are elsewhere?

That scarecrow picked the short straw!

138) What does a turkey say right after another turkey sneezes?

Gob-bless you!

139) What do you use to tie a macaroni necklace together with?

String cheese!

140) What do sweet potatoes do before going to bed?

They put on their yammies!

141) What has feathers and webbed feet?

A Turkey wearing scuba flippers!

142) What do you get when you mix a pumpkin, a pirate and a pilgrim?

A squash-buckler!

143) What kind of glaze do monsters love with their turkey?

Francranberry glaze!

144) What do you get when you cross a turkey with a harp?

A turkey that can pluck itself!

145) Why are caramel apples so friendly with one other?

They like sticking together!

146) How do turkeys stay physically fit?

With daily egg-cercise!

147) What do you get when you overcook your Thanksgiving potatoes?

Ashed Potatoes!

148) Where do beans invest their money?

In the stalk market!

149) Why are the kids eating dried grapes on Thanksgiving day?

Because they are raisin' awareness!

150) What is the worst punishment a turkey can get in a game of basketball?

A technical fowl!

151) What is the best fast food a kid can get on Thanksgiving?

Turkey Nuggets!

152) What did the kitty say after eating a whole Thanksgiving meal?

I ate too meow-uch!

153) Why was the cheese very confident in the kitchen?

Because it thought it was grater than everything else!

154) What kind of facial expression do pilgrims make when they are in pain?

A pil-grimacing face!

155) What is the cheapest way to drive to Grandma's house for Thanksgiving?

The freeway!

156) What should you wear before you walk into a Thanksgiving dinner?

A har-vest!

157) Where do turkeys commonly dance?

At the butterball!

158) What did the corn husk say to the other corn husk when telling a secret?

Come ear!

159) How did the cranberries get wet?

They were Ocean Sprayed!

160) What is the rare ingredient pilgrims use to bake cookies?

May-flour!

161) What kinds of people do turkeys love the most?

Vegetarians!

162) Why is it hard to stop telling Thanksgiving jokes?

Because it is not easy to simply quit cold turkey!

163) What did the scarecrow win an award for?

For being out-standing in its field.

164) How do you make a turkey float?

Just serve the turkey with root beer and ice cream on the side!

165) Why do elderly people normally get cramps after a Thanksgiving dinner?

Because they eat too many crampberries

166) Where do the pilgrims take the mayflower when it needs a checkup?

To the nearest doc!

167) What happens when lots of pumpkins gather around a vegetable patch?

Election day for the next pumpking!

168) How are large pumpkins in pumpkin patches normally rewarded?

By getting a spot at a Thanksgiving dinner table!

169) What do you call a table with no meat?

A vege-table!

170) What do you call a trembling turkey?

A jerky turkey!

171) If April showers bring mayflowers, what do Mayflowers bring?

Pilgrims silly!

172) Why do young students get low grades after Thanksgiving Day?

Because after the holidays, everything gets marked down!

173) What do parents normally make if they don't have time to cook for Thanksgiving?

A restaurant reservation!

174) What is a pumpkin's favorite extreme sport?

Bungee gourd jumping!

175) What happens when you eat too much turkey on Thanksgiving?

You start to crave for the pumpkin pie!

Chapter 3: Knock-Knock Jokes

"Over and over I marvel at the blessings of my life: Each year has grown better than the last." ~ Lawrence Welk

1) Knock, knock!

Who's there?

Arthur.

Arthur who?

Arthur any Thanksgiving leftovers?

2) Knock, knock!

Who's there?

Tamara.

Tamara who?

Tamara I'm finally going to go cold turkey!

3) Knock, knock!

Who's there?

Norma Lee.

Norma Lee who?

Norma Lee I don't stuff myself up this much!

4) Knock, knock!

Who's there?

Don.

Don who?

Don just stand there! Start stuffing the turkey!

5) Knock, knock!

Who's there?

Seth.

Seth who?

Seth the table because Thanksgiving dinner is ready to serve!

6) Knock, knock!

Who's there?

Howie.

Howie who?

Howie long will this giant turkey take to fully cook?

7) Knock, knock!

Who's there?

Mike.

Mike who?

Mike me some pumpkin pie pretty please!

8) Knock, knock!

Who's there?

Harry.

Harry who?

Harry up! I'm starving for some turkey!

9) Knock, knock!

Who's there?

Gladys.

Gladys who?

Gladys finally Thanksgiving Day!

10) Knock, knock!

Who's there?

Annie.

Annie who?

Annie more pumpkin pie leftovers in the fridge?

11) Knock, knock!

Who's there?

Washington.

Washington who?

Washington all these dishes is the worst part of the day after Thanksgiving is over!

12) Knock, knock!

Who's there?

Theresa.

Theresa who?

Theresa's more than enough Turkey and stuffing for everyone!

13) Knock, knock!

Who's there?

Canoe.

Canoe who?

Can-oe help me chase this wild turkey?

14) Knock, knock!

Who's there?

Barry.

Barry who?

Barry fruit punch is what will make my cranberry-glazed turkey meal complete!

15) Knock, knock!

Who's there?

Alma.

Alma who?

Al-ma Thanksgiving dinner is gone! Whodunnit?!

16) Knock, knock!

Who's there?

Izza.

Izza who?

Izza-always nice to see all of our relatives get together on Thanksgiving Day!

17) Knock, knock!

Who's there?

Rome.

Rome who?

Rome around with me to find some Thanksgiving leftovers!

18) Knock, knock!

Who's there?

Sid.

Sid who?

Sid down and finish all of your turkey before you move on to dessert

19) Knock, knock!

Who's there?

Possum.

Possum who?

Po-ssum gravy on that turkey so you can taste the awesomeness!

20) Knock, knock!

Who's there?

Aldo.

Aldo who?

Al-do anything for another bite of your pumpkin pie!

21) Knock, knock!

Who's there?

Wilma.

Wilma who?

Wil Ma be preparing the Thanksgiving meal or taking out food?

22) Knock, knock!

Who's there?

Levi.

Levi who?

Levi some space on your turkey plate for the stuffing, mashed potatoes and other Thanksgiving yum yums!

23) Knock, knock!

Who's there?

Aida.

Aida who?

Aida-lot of mashed potatoes and Thanksgiving stuffing!

24) Knock, knock!

Who's there?

Phillip.

Philip who?

Phill-ip your plate with the largest turkey piece!

25) Knock, knock!

Who's there?

Abbott.

Abbott who?

Abbott time we try the cornbread stuffing!

26) Knock, knock!

Who's there?

Luke.

Luke who?

Luke at all this food we need to finish by ourselves!

27) Knock, knock!

Who's there?

General Lee.

General Lee who?

General Lee I like my turkey with extra gravy!

28) Knock, knock!

Who's there?

Xavier.

Xavier who?

Xavier some spaghetti squash!

29) Knock, knock!

Who's there?

Juicy.

Juicy who?

Jui-cy how that cranberry sauce perfectly glazes that turkey?

30) Knock, knock!

Who's there?

Ester.

Ester who?

Es-ter anymore mashed potatoes left?

31) Knock, knock!

Who's there?

Fonda.

Fonda who?

I'm very Fonda that herb roasted turkey you prepared last night!

32) Knock, knock!

Who's there?

Brie.

Brie who?

Brie me another plate right now!

33) Knock, knock!

Who's there?

Avery.

Avery who?

Avery-one loves the Thanksgiving butternut squash salad!

34) Knock, knock!

Who's there?

Harper.

Harper who?

Harper Thanksgiving to everyone in attendance here!

35) Knock, knock!

Who's there?

Ken.

Ken who?

Ken you see that fat turkey in the oven?

36) Knock, knock!

Who's there?

Watson.

Watson who?

Watson this year's Thanksgiving Day parade?

37) Knock, knock!

Who's there?

Wyatt.

Wyatt who?

Wyatt is taking so long for all the leaves to fall?

38) Knock, knock!

Who's there?

Nadia.

Nadia who?

Nadia head if you care more about the stuffing than the turkey!

39) Knock, knock!

Who's there?

Enid.

Enid who?

Enid a bigger oven to fit this huge turkey!

40) Knock, knock!

Who's there?

Percy.

Percy who?

Percy me the cranberry sauce please!

41) Knock, knock!

Who's there?

Rosemary.

Rosemary who?

Rosemary can be added to turkeys too and not just chickens!

42) Knock, knock!

Who's there?

Gus.

Gus who?

Gus I'm going to celebrate two Thanksgiving days this year because of all this food!

43) Knock, knock!

Who's there?

Hans.

Hans who?

Hans off those Turkey drumsticks but you can have the breasts!

44) Knock, knock!

Who's there?

Lettuce.

Lettuce who?

Lettuce make some room for some Thanksgiving veggies too!

45) Knock, knock!

Who's there?

Lion.

Lion who?

Lion on your doormat waiting for Thanksgiving pet treats!

46) Knock, knock!

Who's there?

Turnip.

Turnip who?

Turnip the oven to 350 degrees for the juiciest Thanksgiving turkey!

47) Knock, knock!

Who's there?

Robin.

Robin who?

Robin all your Thanksgiving food! Bwa hah hah!

48) Knock, knock!

Who's there?

Water.

Water who?

Water you waiting for? The sparkling cranberry punch is ready to drink!

49) Knock, knock!

Who's there?

Pecan.

Pecan who?

Pecan a pie for your own size!

50) Knock, knock!

Who's there?

Duncan.

Duncan who?

Duncan your turkeys before they hatch!

Chapter 4: Situations

"Homemade stuffing is my favorite thing about Thanksgiving. I wish people served it more than just once a year" ~ Troy Gentile

1. **"I made a huge Thanksgiving dinner for guests from all over town.**

I spent countless hours dabbling with recipes I found.

But the turkey, unfortunately didn't cook golden brown.

Worst of all, I cooked the turkey upside down!"

2. On a lazy afternoon, a student was asked to write a short essay on what to be thankful for this coming Thanksgiving Day.

The student smiled as he wrote, "I'm thankful I'm not a turkey!"

3. **One day, a ship full of pilgrims landed on an island full of peace-loving turkeys.**

Most of the pilgrims thought it was a great place to rest but one pilgrim thought of an idea to make dinner more interesting.

The pilgrim said, "Maybe we can have one of the turkeys for dinner!"

The other pilgrims agreed and that one pilgrim approached the turkey.

The turkey greeted, "Gobble! Gobble!" and flapped its wings as if it is waving hello.

The pilgrim smiled as he noticed how fat the turkey was

Moments later, the pilgrims started to say "Gobble! Gobble!" too as they enjoyed the freshly cooked turkey and feeling very thankful!

4. Every Thanksgiving one passionate mother really enjoys preparing her delicious stuffing for the turkey.

This Thanksgiving was no different and everyone in her family knows how delicious it is to the point that they ate very little breakfast and snacks.

Understandably, everyone is very hungry and after a long wait the Thanksgiving feast is ready to serve for all.

But there is someone on the dining table that is not hungry and completely full...

... It's the turkey. He's completely stuffed!

5. A father and his son were about to have their Thanksgiving dinner.

The son suddenly asked, "Why does the president pardon a turkey every year? It's a waste of good meat!"

The father replied, "It's a gesture of goodwill. There is a saying, it is the little things that count!"

The father then got up to get some stuffing while his son went ahead and served himself some delicious turkey. He took a lot of food and only left small pieces of turkey.

The father asked, "Why is your plate so full and I get only a few small pieces?"

The son responded, "But I thought it's the little things that count!"

6. A mother asked his three boys to help fix Thanksgiving dinner.

The eldest boy said, ""Okay. Will prepare the table!""

The middle child said, "Really? The Thanksgiving dinner is broken?"

The youngest child said, "Yeah! Why fix what isn't broken?"

7. A young kid was watching his grandmother prepare his Thanksgiving meal. This is the first time ever he is seeing how Thanksgiving is prepared since his mom wouldn't share it.

"What are you doing?", the kid asked.

"Stuffing the turkey.", the grandmother replied.

The kid said, "Cool! Are you going to hang that next to the deer?"

8. On the first week of November, one brave turkey decided to consult a fortune teller.

He told the fortune teller, "Tell me my future!"

The fortune teller looked at her crystal ball and paused shaking her head.

"What do you see?", the concerned turkey asked.

The fortune teller only uttered a single word, "Leftovers!"

9. Many turkeys panicked on November because they still recall what happened last year when so many of them ended on dinner plates.

One turkey, however, came up with a bright idea to save his friends - get into the t-shirt making business!

The turkey was a talented artist being able to make convincing skinny pictures turkey bodies.

The t-shirts sold like hotcakes and the turkey finally ran out of stock.

But there was one problem... the turkey forgot to keep one for himself!

10. A young boy walked into a doctor's office. He had a carrot stuck up his nostril,

a banana in one ear and a potato in the other ear.

The boy asked the doctor, "Can you do something for me?"

The doctor replied, ""Well, how about I teach you how to eat more sensibly?""

The boy then said, "Oh no, I did this on a dare."

The doctor sighed and said, "Ahhh then there is no hope for you."

Fun Thanksgiving Riddles
&
Trick Questions
For Kids and Family

Turkey Stuffing Edition

300 Riddles and Brain Teasers That Kids and Family Will Enjoy!

Riddleland

Introduction

"A thankful heart is not only the greatest virtue, but the parent of all the other virtues." ~ Cicero

We would like to personally thank you for purchasing this book. **Fun Thanksgiving Riddles and Trick Questions for Kids and Family!** book is a collection of 300 fun brain teasers and riddles of easy to hard difficulty.

These brain teasers will challenge the children and their parents to think and stretch their minds. They have also many other benefits such as:

- **Bonding** – It is an excellent way for parents and their children to spend some quality time and create some fun and memorable memories.

- **Confidence Building -** When parents give the riddles, it creates a safe environment for children to burst out answers even if they are incorrect. This helps the children to develop self confidence in expressing themselves.

- **Improve Vocabulary** – Riddles are usually written in advance words, therefore children will need to understand these words before they can share the riddles.

- **Better reading comprehension** – Many children can read at a young age but may not understand the context of the sentences. Riddles can help develop the children's interest to comprehend the context before they can share it to their friends.

- **Sense of humor** –Funny creative riddles can help children develop their sense of humor while getting their brains working.

Chapter 1: Easy Riddles

"If you want to turn your life around, try thankfulness. It will change your life mightily." – Gerald Good

1. Inside a turkey

I am what people often love eating the most. I don't get cold because I stay warm inside of the turkey. What am I?

2. Rich Holiday

I am a special day, and I fall in between two other holidays. I come with bountiful feasts, thanks all around and have a rich history of how America came to be. What holiday am I?

3. Main course

I am the main course of every Thanksgiving meal. I am the symbol of the holiday. What am I?

4. Turkey sidekick

I am the turkey's little sidekick. If the turkey is the main symbol of Thanksgiving, I may just be a close second. I am several little yellow kernels arranged in a row. What am I known as?

5. Thanksgiving evening

What is always full on Thanksgiving evening?

6. Hot Thanksgiving

What is always hot on Thanksgiving?

7. Guaranteed on Thanksgiving

What is guaranteed to be on the dining table on Thanksgiving?

8. Baked and delicious

I am a special dish, baked and delicious. I am cooked inside a deep pan and served in it also. I can come in a variety of forms. What am I?

9. Safe turkey

When does a wild turkey know it's safe?

10. Cranberry mess

A can of cranberry sauce falls on the floor fully intact. How will you clean up the mess?

11. Cooked Turkey

Hi, I am a cooked turkey that weighs about 10 pounds. How long will it take to defrost me?

12. Cob tool

There is a can of corn that will be used to make corn casserole. What is the best tool to use in order to take the kernels off the cob?

13. Corn on the head

How do you know that a piece of corn won't fall out of a tree and hit you on the head?

14. A spud's cousin

Another well-liked vegetable, popular on this day. Full of carbs, some protein, and many things you can say. People think I am interesting because my cousin's name is Spud. But many things can be done with me, so no, I am not a dud. What am I?

15. Always have room

Something that's part of the dinner but not a part of the main meal. It follows the main meal with sweetness and people always have room for it, no matter how full they are. Did you save room for this? What is it?

16. No chance

Outdoor decorations don't stand a chance when I am around. Put them outside while I am going on and I will blow them away. If I am strong enough, I may blow you away also. What am I?

17. Favorite dessert

Pumpkin season is over, but lucky for you, you can still use the insides of this wonderful vegetable to make me. I am your favorite dessert on Thanksgiving night. What dessert am I?

18. Turkey fight

The part of the turkey you can grip in your hand. Many people will fight over it at the dinner table as there are usually just a couple. What are they?

19. Laugh and cry

I am who you gather with around the dinner table. We laugh, we cry, we love each other tremendously and enjoy a bountiful feast. Who am I?

20. Keep up the pants

When is corn used to keep someone's pants up?

21. Eating your food quickly

I am what is going on when you eat your food quickly and with little regard to what is around you. Perhaps, this is why a turkey is constantly saying this as they are watching all of us chow down on our meals. What am I?

22. Turkey race

If two turkeys are standing at the front door facing into the house and they want to race to see who leaves the house first, who would win if the first turkey runs towards the back door at 25 miles per hour and the second turkey turns around and runs 5 miles per hours?

23. Uneaten meal

I am a big part of your holiday dinner. You will have me at the table to eat, but you will never eat me. What am I?

24. Number of pies

A pie is cut into eight slices. There are seven people at the dinner table. How many slices of pie are left?

25. Favorite baked starch

Everyone's favorite bread on the table. Soft and moist, ready and able to fill you up no problem indeed. Don't eat too many, or there will be no room for turkey. What am I?

26. American sport

A popular American sport you can watch, even on Thanksgiving. I start with a kick and end when the fourth quarter is over. What sport am I?

27. A fruit dish

I am a common side dish made from a dark red fruit. If you're in a pinch, you can get me from a can. What am I?

28. Late meal

A friend arrives late to Thanksgiving dinner after all the food has been eaten. What can you give them to eat?

29. The popular person

The most popular person on Thanksgiving Day. Without me, there would be no Thanksgiving feast. Who am I?

30. Carving a turkey

The Turkey is completely cooked in the oven and ready to carve. I go to the table with my carving knife. I realize that I am not yet ready to carve the turkey. What am I missing?

31. Sad cranberry

What do you call a cranberry that is sad?

32. Last piece of turkey

Carter saw the last piece of the turkey. No one was going for it, so he grabbed it. Finishing off the turkey for good. No one else was eating at this time. A couple of minutes later, he looked over and saw his brother eating a piece of turkey. He did not have one before. How did this happen?

33. Favorite time

What's everyone's favorite time on Thanksgiving?

34. Room for turkey

You are looking at a turkey on a platter. The turkey covers the whole platter and there is no room on it for anything else. Yet, when you look at this platter, you also see stuffing. How is this possible?

35. Cooking turkeys

If you have five turkeys and you cook two of them. How many do you have left?

36. Won't drink

I am on your table for drinking, but you won't drink me. What am I?

37. Turkey Meat

What kind of meat is Turkey?

38. People, floats and music

While you gather in your home, others gather to showcase on the street. People, floats and loud music echo in the streets. What is this called?

39. New settlers

All the new settlers that came to this land are cheering at the same time. They are all standing together in one place. What is this called?
We come from them. Who are they?

40. The famous spice

Traditions were followed by people long before. Those that came here in search of newer things. They produced what they could, and they produced us. We come from them. Who are they?

41. Turkey emotions

What did the stuffing say to the turkey to help it realize that he understood his emotions?

42. Knocked down

What happens when a turkey gets knocked down?

43. Corn base

I am the base from which corn grows and create many of your favorite foods. What am I?

44. Baking ingredient

I am a necessary ingredient for many of the things we bake. However, in order for me to work properly, I must be broken first. What am I?

45. Staying awake

Johnny wants to stay up all day on Thanksgiving. What is the best way for him to do it?

46. Warm drink

Curl up with this warm drink on a cold night. Add some marshmallows for texture. What drink is it?

47. Piling leaves

Those multicolored leaves look beautiful and all, but as time goes by, they will fall, creating a giant mess on the lawn. They need to be picked up, but first, they need to be piled in one location with the help of me. What am I?

48. Acorn and leaves

The trees in Mike's front yard have twice as many leaves as acorns. If the maple tree has 50 leaves, how many acorns will it have?

49. Slip and slide

How do you turn a turkey into a slip and slide?

50. Vegetable currency

This starchy yellow vegetable was so valuable during the days of the settlers that it was often used just like money to trade for goods and services. What was it?

51. Messy potato

I am a potato, but I am soft. You don't eat me by holding me, but you must use a spoon. If you use your hands, you will create a mess. What am I?

52. No feather turkey

What do you call a turkey that has no feathers?

53. Boiled corn

If you have three pieces of corn and boil two, how many do you have left?

54. Name not on Thanksgiving

On Thanksgiving, you can call a person the wrong name, but never call them this?

55. Sea thanksgiving course

A delicious entrée. The main course at Thanksgiving. But also, the name of a country across the sea. What am I?

56. Common Food

What does all the food on Thanksgiving have in common?

57. A charged turkey

Why would a turkey get arrested? What would be the charge?

58. Plant turkey

If turkeys came from a plant, what would it be called?

59. Food in a container

A word that can mean an actual food or the container it is put in. What is it?

60. Turkey night

There are two turkeys talking on a farm on Thanksgiving morning. One is expecting a long and boring night at the barn reading. The other one was invited to a special dinner where he is expected to be the center of attention. Which one's night will go better?

61. Drink from butter

Something that you drink out of that's made from butter. What is it?

62. Turkey meat

If a turkey bone weighs one pound, how much does the meat weigh?

63. Dessert bread

How did the husband kindly ask his wife for bread in a loving way, while also turning the phrase into a dessert?

64. Thanksgiving ride

What is large and decorative, riding down the street, with wheels that you will only see on Thanksgiving?

65. Month after spooks before joy

I am the month that comes after some spooks and scares, but before some jolly good times. What month am I?

66. Cooking smell

The name of a heavenly smell that fills the home when you are cooking. What is this called?

67. Funny turkeys

A group of turkeys making fun of each other. What is it known as?

68. Turkey or cornstalk

Who would win a race between a turkey and a cornstalk?

69. Turkey talk

Why is it easy to talk to a turkey?

70. The fifth course

A household is expecting a very large gathering on thanksgiving. They make a total of four different main courses. From left to right, they are 1) a ham, 2), a turkey, 3) another ham, 4) another turkey. What is the fifth course?

71. Insane giblets

Why are giblets always doing insane things?

72. Something colorful

I come in different colors. I can be food, or I can be ornamental. I am long, grow on a stick, and have hundreds of kernels all in a row. What am I?

73. Outdoor flames

People gather around and watch my controlled flames. I keep them warm; I keep them talking, and I keep them comfortable. Don't place me indoors, or I will create much damage. What am I?

74. Turkey won't fly

You bring your pet turkey indoors because it is raining outside. How do you know it won't fly away with your stuff?

75. See me in a wild turkey

What do you not want to see on a cooked turkey that you would on a wild turkey?

76. Edible bean

I am an edible bean, but I also care about the environment. What am I called?

77. Cooking, cleaning, hanging

I am used with cooking, but I do not cook. I keep your clothes clean, but I do not wash. I hang from your neck, sometime fashionably, but I am not a necklace. What am I?

78. Cooked meal

On Thanksgiving Day, a feast could not be prepared, because everyone in the family had to work. The mom worked at the hospital. The father worked at the store. The son was teaching at the high school. The daughter was waitressing at a restaurant. When they came home, a meal was prepared for them on the table. Who cooked it for them?

79. Stolen food

When the family arrived home on a cold day on Thanksgiving, they discovered all of their food was gone. Everyone had solid alibis. Johnny was mowing the lawn; Allison was getting groceries and Sarah was at a friend's house. Who likely ate the food?

80. Turkey aboard plane

A man and his turkey are trying to board a plane. The man has a small duffel bag. The turkey has a large suitcase. Why was the turkey not allowed on the plane?

81. Potato peeling time

It took Tim 10 minutes to peel eight potatoes for Thanksgiving dinner. How long will it take him to peel Two?

82. Fit one on freezer

Susan buys turkey, two bottles of soda and a tub of ice cream the day before thanksgiving. Only one of the three items will fit into the freezer. How will Susan handle this?

83. Thanksgiving birthday

Tim's birthday one year happened four days before Thanksgiving. The next year, it was three days before Thanksgiving. The year after that, it was two days before Thanksgiving. Finally, the year after that, it was on Thanksgiving itself. How did this occur?

84. Flying turkey in Atlantic

If a turkey can run 20 miles per hour, how fast can they fly across the Atlantic Ocean?

85. Corn street

There is a long road in a neighborhood where all of the corn live. What is this street called?

86. Turkey and ostrich race

If a turkey is running from Massachusetts to California going west at 20 miles per hours, and an ostrich is running East at 40 miles per hour, who will reach California first?

87. Pilgrim voyage

How long did it take for the Pilgrims to do a 20-day voyage?

88. Seating arrangement

A husband and wife couple have exactly 10 guests coming over for Thanksgiving. They place exactly 10 chairs around the table, including two main chairs at each end. After all of the guests have taken a seat at the table, where will the husband and wife sit?

89. Legged food carrier

I will carry food, but I have no arms. I have legs, but do not walk. I will showcase food but will not serve it to you. What am I?

90. Two more drumsticks

The turkeys made for dinner generally just have two drumsticks. Both Johnny and Adam eat two drumsticks each at the dinner. How did this happen?

91. Thanksgiving sandwich

The most popular sandwich after Thanksgiving. What is it?

92. Roasting time

It took 3 hours to roast a turkey at 350 degrees. How long will it take to roast the same turkey at 300 degrees?

93. Food commander

What food on the Thanksgiving table will be best at commanding an army?

94. Meat preference

People are picky. They usually have a preference as to which part of the turkey they want to eat. What is the biggest argument over as far as the meat of the turkey?

95. Pilgrim location

How did the Pilgrims know that they found a solid location?

96. After Thanksgiving

I come to you after Thanksgiving. I last until the weekend. People get excited when they hear about me. I am there all day and all night. What am I?

97. Cornfield day

As a corn farmer walks through his fields day after day, what is the one thing that will always go up and never come down?

98. Nutty snack

I am protein filled and make a great snack. Some people are afraid of me because I am a little nutty. I am smooth and brown and may go into one of your favorite pies. What am I?

99. No turkey, no entry

There is a store that only allows you to come in if you are with a turkey. One day, two birds walk into the store together, and one of them is not a turkey. The store still let them in. Why is that?

100. Boring rock

I may seem boring to some, but I have quite a past. I helped start a country. I welcomed the Pilgrims. In the end though, I am just your everyday rock. What am I?

101. Snow clearing time

You get an unexpected snowstorm on Thanksgiving. You want to clear the driveway before your guests arrive. If it takes you about 5 minutes to clear 10 square feet of snow on the driveway. How long will it take you to clear 30 square feet of melted snow?

102. Thanksgiving groceries

Myron drives to three different stores to get groceries for Thanksgiving dinner. When he arrives home, he only has bags from one store. Why is that?

103. Thanksgiving dinners

Bill was at three different Thanksgiving dinners. He only drove to two different houses. How did he do it?

104. Time zone matters

Mikey lives on Pacific Standard Time, which is three hours behind Eastern Standard Time. He wants to order his mother a gift and in order for it to arrive before Thanksgiving, he has to order it by 8 PM EST. What time does he have to order it by?

105. Blood is thicker than water

A turkey meets two other turkeys, one with light feathers and one with dark feathers. One of them is a possible family member. How will the turkey know which one?

Chapter 2: Hard Riddles

"Appreciation can change a day, even change a life. Your willingness to put it into words is all that is necessary." ~ Margaret Cousins

106. Spiced up turkey

Turkey is often too dry, but I add some moistness, taste, and texture. What am I?

107. Working shift

Jamie is working a 12-hour shift on Thanksgiving. Her shift starts at 6 PM and finishes at 6 AM. How did this occur?

108. Turkey carver

If Mike took ten minutes to carve a turkey, how fast could Phil, who is a champion turkey carver in New York, do it?

109. Spell out the N

Thanksgiving is quite a long word. Want it to be shorter? Try spelling it with no "N"

110. Stay on turkey's butt

If three people are walking behind a turkey and want to stay behind it, how fast do they have to go to pass it?

111. Grandma's corn

Carol was walking to her Grandmother's house to give her five pieces of corn that she needed. While carrying seven pieces, she ate two during the walk. How many corns short was she by the time she arrived at her grandma's house?

112. Knocked out by punch

Jenny has Thanksgiving dinner at her house and since the city water had become contaminated, she decides to have other drinks instead. There is a newly made bowl of punch on the table filled with ice. Jenny drinks a glass and she feels fine. Mike drinks another glass right afterwards, and he feels fine too. 15 minutes later, Kayla drinks a glass and she starts feeling sick. Mike is curious so he drinks a little bit more, and this time, he becomes sick also. What happened?

113. Through thick or thin

You are at the dinner table. You have a match and need to light two candles. One candle is thicker and may take longer to light than the other. Which do you light first?

114. Toasted selection

I am an amazing selection of food. I am also a term used for what you apply to a piece of toast. What am I?

115. Brine it up

How long should you brine a cooked turkey that is about 12 pounds?

116. Post-Christmas thanksgiving

When you're here, Thanksgiving will occur after Christmas. Where are you?

117. Historical song

What was created after the first Thanksgiving that is also the name of a popular animated song?

118. Guilty feet got rhythm

A pile of feathers was found on the scene where something was stolen. They have two turkeys who are possible suspects. How do they know which turkey is the guilty one?

119. Smorgasbord

The dinner was quite a smorgasbord. Now spell that properly.

120. Crack the egg

Is it best to break a cracked egg using the counter or a spoon?

121. Kernel corn

How many kernels does a corn husk have?

122. Pumpkin pies

Your friend's mom makes two pumpkin pies. The first one is whole while the second one is half eaten with four slices left. Which one has more slices?

123. Potato skin

After cutting a peeled potato, is it easier to remove the skin before? or after boiling it?

124. Corn maze in the making

A corn maze is made from thousands of corns. But how many pieces of corn does it actually take to make one?

125. Corn not found

Corn is delicious and plentiful. It is found on every continent on the planet, except that one icy place way down south. Where is corn not found?

126. Tree spice

I'm a common spice, and I make everything nice. Find me on rolls, find me in tea. Just know one thing, I come from trees. What am I?

127. Turkey Thursday

James comes into town with his turkey Thursday, stays three days and leaves with his turkey Thursday. How did he do it?

128. Library book race

Jane leaves on Thanksgiving morning to go to the library to check out a book. James will leave an hour later to get to the library for the same book. Who will get the book first?

129. Veggie bread to go

A delicious bread made from a starchy vegetable. Yellow in color, baked, and I am ready to go. What am I?

130. Sea transporter

I carried the people that would ultimately come to the new land. I crossed great seas, witnessed great illness. Not everyone who started made it to the end. But those who did, were part of the first thanksgiving. What am I?

131. The ancestors

The first settlers came to start a great tradition and make their own great additions. Who were they?

132. Nutty pie

A delicious pie made from a hearty nut, baked to perfection to make it gooey and warm. It will settle in your stomach nicely. What am I?

133. Purple potato

A purple looking treat that feels like a potato, but it is actually sweet. You may confuse it with a sweet potato. What is it?

134. Broken wishbone

If you break a wishbone in half when you make a wish, how many wishbones do you have?

135. Thanksgiving birthday

Johnny was feeling kind of bummed out. His birthday was on a Thursday, on November 29th. To his dismay, his birthday did not fall on Thanksgiving, even though it was the last Thursday of the month. Why is this?

136. Turkey goes North

A turkey walks across the street going North and it takes about 20 seconds. How long will it take to cross the road again going in the same direction?

137. Clean up the crumbs

When you're devouring your food, some may get on your lips. You may use this to clean up the crumbs. What is it?

138. Pilgrim ship builders

If one Pilgrim built a ship in 12 days. How long will it take two Pilgrims to build the same ship?

139. Better on the inside

Even though I don't go on top of the turkey and am stuffed inside it, certain parts of the country call me this. What am I?

140. Turkey alternative

A common entree found alongside the turkey, for those who may not like turkey. What am I??

141. Turkey part taken out

I am a part of the turkey but not eaten with the turkey. I know how the turkey feels on the inside. Take me out before you bake. I can be eaten with other things too. What am I?

142. Couple champions

The turkey was part of a couple's dance competition. He won a gold medal. What did his partner win?

143. Household disguise

If a turkey wanted to disguise itself as a household item, what could it be?

144. Cider weight

How many pounds of cider will an empty eight-ounce glance have in it?

145. Long but short prayer

Mary's grandparents began praying on Thanksgiving at 11:55. They prayed for 10 minutes, and when they were done, it was 12:05 the next day. How is this possible?

146. Turkey runners

If two turkeys begin running in opposite directions from the same starting point, both going at speeds of 10 miles per hour, how long will it take them to reach the same spot.

147. The grateful dad

The always grateful dad sat down for Thanksgiving dinner. The turkey was cold, the stuffing was soggy, and the pie was too sweet. Why did the dad not complain?

148. A great dinner

There are so many things that make up a great Thanksgiving dinner. But what is the main key to it?

149. Traffic Overpass

The turkey crosses an empty overpass during heavy traffic. How was he able to get past the cars?

150. Ornamental horn

I am filled with fruit, but not a tree. I am shaped like a horn, but I am not found on an animal. I am ornamental, but I am not being hung. I am overflowing, but I don't look messy. What am I?

151. Alpha and omega

I am at the start of Thanksgiving, will appear at the end of night and will occur again at the beginning of tomorrow. What am I?

152. Shy turkey

Why was the turkey shy?

153. Mothers know best

How did mom know that everyone loved the stuffing?

154. Uncontrollable turkey

What is a turkey that is out of control?

155. East to West end

One turkey runs into a store on the West end, while another turkey goes inside on the East end. Who reached the inside first?

156. Popular month

How did the turkey know it was so popular during the month of November?

157. Tom Turkey

What did everyone call Tom Turkey after he lost his hat?

158. Apple pie on granny's house

You are going to a party at both of your grandparent's house. At the first house, they have one apple pie. At the next house, they have two apple pies. How many will be at the third house?

159. Solo corn

What do you call one piece of corn on the table?

160. College turkey

What did the turkey want to study at college to better understand himself?

161. Movie in a row

Two turkeys walk into a 10-row movie theatre. They are sitting in the second row from the top. Which row are they sitting in?

162. Turkey party

Where can a turkey truly get down and dance the night away?

163. Ready-made pie

Your mom buys a ready-made apple pie from the store. How long will it take to cook?

164. American potluck

When was America's first potluck?

165. Evil turkey

Why did the turkey look so evil on the outside?

166. Thrown away bone

What did the man say when he threw his turkey bone away?

167. Four heads

What do you call the heads of four families sitting at a dinner table?

168. Eat all turkey can

Why did the turkey eat all of the food on his plate at once?

169. Autumn leaves

Steve saw 10 autumn leaves that fell from the tree on the ground. He collected five leaves from the tree to add to his centerpiece. How many leaves are left on the ground?

170. American pie

I don't come from pumpkins, and I don't come from nuts. I come from a tree and will be pie number three for dessert. I guess you can say I am as American as me. What am I?

171. Corn made

Made from the starchy vegetable you love to see when running through a corn-maze. Cooked in a deep pan. Ready as soon as you take it out of the oven. What am I?

172. Longing to eat shortly

Tommy began eating leftover thanksgiving dinner on a late November night. He finished eating this dinner in December. How did he do it?

173. Lucky 13 guests

There was a total of 10 chairs around the dinner table. There were 13 guests at the Thanksgiving dinner. Everybody was able to sit. How is this possible?

174. Visiting hours

Jimmy has to go to three different houses on Thanksgiving. He spends a total of two and a half hours between the three houses. The third house he goes to, he spends half the amount of time at than he did at the first two houses, both of which he spends an equal amount of time at. How long did he spend at each house?

175. Pumpkin sometimes

A common vegetable used for cooking many things on this festive day. Comes in a variety of colors and is often depicted as round and slender. Sometimes a pumpkin, sometimes not. What am I?

176. Tom and John race

Tom leaves to go to his friend's house for Thanksgiving dinner at 4 PM driving 25 mph. John leaves for his friend's house at 4:15 PM driving 35 mph. At what point will John catch up to Tom?

177. The natives

We were the ones already on this land that welcomed the settlers as they got off their ship. We helped make the harvest that would one day always be celebrated. Who are we?

178. Rustling sound

The sound of these rustling outside way up high will bring a calming effect to a beautiful Autumn day. What are they?

179. The fruit picking

Jim picked an apple. Then he picked an orange and then he picked a grape. He found all of these in one spot easily, but he is not in a store. For all three, he had to climb a tree. Where is he?

180. Eat the leftovers

Bobby had leftover turkey, carrots, peas and broth for his dinner. However, he did not eat them separately, but at the same time. What did he have?

181. The sun protection

A Pilgrim never complained about the sun. He had me with my wide brim, dark color and rugged material. With me, the sun never got in his eyes. What am I?

182. Festive feast

The first Thanksgiving feast was filled with food, love and laughter. What was the most important item for them in order to share the food properly?

183. Corn bowls

If two Pilgrims are sitting at a table, how will they evenly split two full bowls of corn between them?

184. Turkey meets pig

What happens when a turkey meets a pig?

185. Rooster lays an egg

A turkey has a rooster friend and he is on top of a barn about to lay an egg. The turkey wants to make sure he catches it, so the egg does not break. After the egg is laid, what side of the barn should the turkey stand on in order to catch the egg?

186. Tickle the turkeys

How do we know that turkeys like to tickle?

187. Turkey carving

If it took Jim 5 minutes to carve a 10-pound turkey with one knife, how long will it take him to carve the same turkey with two knives?

188. National bird

I am a Turkey. I am native to the land that started Thanksgiving. I am so native, that they actually wanted to make me the national bird. The national bird of what country?

189. Help me walk

When the Pilgrims arrived at Plymouth Rock, what did they use to help them walk off the ships?

190. Turkey day

People eat turkey on Thanksgiving. What other days can people eat turkey?

191. Whipped pie

You buy a 20 ounce can of whipped cream from the store. How many pies can you use it on until it is not full anymore?

192. Thanksgiving guests

From 4-8 PM, a total of 20 guests arrived for Thanksgiving festivities. At 5 PM, there were 10 guests. How is this possible?

193. Make seven even

Seven turkeys are doing the turkey trot, how do you make the odd number seven even?

194. Gravy container

A restaurant owner makes a ton of gravy because it is so delicious and gets eaten right away. If he makes 10 batches of gravy, what types of containers are best to store it in?

195. Featherless turkey

What do you call a turkey that loses all of its feathers?

196. Swimming turkey

What does a turkey use when they go swimming?

197. Salty with water

I am salty, but I am not mean. I am used for cooking, but you don't eat me. I bathe the turkey, but I do not clean it. Without water, I am useless. What am I?

198. Primitive expedition

An expedition, similar to the settlers who first arrived in America, went on and named after them too. What is it called?

199. The mothers and daughters

Jane invites three of her friends for Thanksgiving dinner. Two of them are mothers, two of them are daughters and one of them is a grandmother. How is this possible?

200. Sweet potato pie

How many sweet potatoes does it take to make a cooked sweet potato pie?

201. Full bowl of gravy

There is a full bowl of gravy on the table and three people with mashed potatoes on their plates. The first person picks up the bowl of gravy, and when they're done, they pass it to the second person. The second person takes the bowl and when they're done, they pass it to the third person. When the third person gets the bowl, it is still completely full, so he pours all of it onto his mashed potatoes. How come the bowl was still full when it got to the last person?

202. Cooked in group

If the Pilgrims and Native Americans both cooked a turkey, how would it taste?

203. The American wave

How did the Native Americans wave to the new settlers after they arrived?

204. James and Jimmy

Jimmy was walking in a field and he saw one other turkey walking in the field also. James saw two turkeys in the field at the same time. Where did the other turkey come from?

205. The missing turkeys

10 people are in the frozen food section, where there are 10 turkeys left. Seven bought a turkey. Nine are left. How is this possible.

206. Full on Thanksgiving

Can a person ever feel full on Thanksgiving??

207. Herding the buffalos

A Pilgrim is helping his Native American friend herd all of the buffalo into the field. He owns a total of three buffalo. Two of them were herded into the field. How many does he still have?

208. Turkey went to mall

If a turkey walks into a mall, what place does he want to avoid at all costs?

209. The missing 2 hands

When the clock on the wall said 4 PM, the centerpiece was brought out. With all of the guests included, there were a total of 10 hands, but only eight of them were clapping. What was wrong with the other two?

210. Count what's left

Byron has 10 pieces of turkey, he gives two to his friend, keeps three for himself and puts the rest in the fridge. How many pieces of turkey are left?

211. Packets of brine

Brian buys four packets of brine from the store. He reads the instructions and brines four turkeys. He still has two packets of brine left. How did he brine four turkeys?

Chapter 3: Difficult Riddles

"Not what we say about our blessings, but how we use them is the true measure of our thanksgiving." ~ W.T Purkiser

212. Race back home

After Thanksgiving dinner, Mary went to the mall, Suzy went to the bank, and Tommy went to a friend's house. Who will be home the earliest?

213. Neighbor stole the turkey

A turkey was stolen from a house some time during the week while the owner was out of town. The person's neighbor to the right said he was at work when it was stolen. The neighbor to the left said he did not know where he was when it was stolen. Who likely would have taken the turkey?

214. Stolen corn bushels

Tucker was collecting crops from his harvest. He collected two bushels of corn and put them in his car. When he leaves for a couple minutes and comes back, the corn is gone. There are two people near the car, and he suspects one of them stole the corn. How will he know who?

215. Hatched same day

A farmer has a group of turkeys that were all hatched on the same day. Half of them were hatched in Colorado, the other half were hatched in Nebraska. How did this occur?

216. Paralysis after eating

Named after a medical condition. When you've dined too much, and you cannot move. You're stuck on the couch because you feel like you've gained 20 pounds. What do you have?

217. Table complimentary

I compliment the turkey, but I won't overshadow it. I sit on the table and bring in some beauty. I'm probably the only thing not for eating. What am I?

218. Food coma

When you get a food coma, all you want to do is what?

219. Annual soup kitchen

In 2015, Tommy and his family began going to a soup kitchen after dinner to help out. They have done this every year since. What is an event like this called, that is carried out year after year in the same manner?

220. Walks through school bus

Jenna usually walks about 10 minutes to get to her school bus. The day after Thanksgiving, she left five minutes later than usual. How fast will she have to walk in order to get to the school bus at the same time she does every day?

221. Lost Sam

Sam was walking down a lane. He did not know where he was. He saw trees all-around of different varieties. He looked around on the ground. He saw peaches, he saw apples, he saw oranges, and he saw lemons. Where is Sam?

222. Incredible journey

I am a journey, but not just any kind. I am a journey across the sea, to find new lands. I am what the settlers did when they first found America. As they traveled with their ships on the sea, they went on something that is called me. What am I?

223. Wishing stuff

Hold me, feel me, look at me, wish on me. If two of you pull and break me, the one who gets the larger piece, will get their wish to come true. What am I?

224. Thanksgiving dinners

Terry must go to three Thanksgiving dinners. The first one is 10 miles away, the other one is on the other side 15 miles away, and the last one is 8 miles away on the same side as the last. Which direction should he take?

225. Table protector

As you dig into to your Thanksgiving meal, crumbs will fall, drinks will spill. But if I am there, your table will be protected. What am I?

226. Unfinished delicacy

You look in the fridge the day after the holidays, and it will be full of me. I am the drumstick you did not finish. I am pumpkin pie that is half eaten. I am the stuff you will still enjoy. With me, you will have meals for days. What am I?

227. Turkey drummer

A turkey wanted to play the drums, at first, they would not let him, but then they noticed these. What did they notice?

228. Pilgrim sailors

Hypothetically, if it took the Pilgrims about two months to sail across the Atlantic, how long would it take to sail back in the same direction?

229. Pilgrims arrived

How did the Pilgrims land when they first arrived?

230. May flowers

April showers may bring May flowers, but what do May flowers bring?

231. Pecans on maple trees

Billy needs some pecans for his pies. He has three maple trees in his backyard. Each tree has 10 branches. Each branch can hold up to 20 pecans. He needs about 15 pecans for each pie. How many pies can he make with the pecans on his maple trees?

232. Turkey – pumpkin race

Who would win in a race between a turkey and a pumpkin?

233. Carving the drumstick

If it takes 5 minutes to carve a whole turkey, how long will it take to just carve the drumstick, which is about 1/8 of the size of the whole turkey?

234. Favorite turkey part

James, Tom, and Michael all have their favorite parts of the turkey. James loves the inside; Tom loves the outside, and Michael loves the instruments. What is their favorite part of the turkey?

235. To read or to shop?

James decides to go to the library to do some reading after Thanksgiving dinner. Tom is going shopping to buy some things. Who is making the better decision?

236. All dressed up

Michael and his wife sit down for thanksgiving turkey dinner. It is just the two of them sitting down, but three of them are dressed up. How is this possible?

237. Feast in a house

Two turkeys are standing on one side of the road. One turkey notices a feast in the house across the street. He crosses over and goes inside the house. What kept the other turkey from crossing the street?

238. Carved out pumpkins

Jack has two carved out pumpkins from Halloween. He wants to make pies for Thanksgiving with the inside seeds. How many pies will he be able to make?

239. Turkey race

If two turkeys crossed the street at the same time, which one reached the end first?

240. Last hat standing

A Pilgrim is talking to a Native American. They both sat down and put their respective hats on a table. They agreed that whoever puts their hat on last, eats first. The Pilgrim and Native American are sitting next to each other a few hours later. Both are still hungry and are wearing their respective hats. Who won the contest?

241. Bright in the sky

I am round and orange, but I am not a fruit. I am in the sky, but I do not fly. I am full, but I did not eat. I am bright, but I have no lights. Despite my name, there is nothing you must gather. Just gaze at me with your eyes. What am I?

242. "Hey" everyone

Everyone at the dinner table said "Hey," one after another before they started eating. What was this process called?

243. The giant pot

Nanna had a giant pot that could melt almost anything thrown in there. It absorbed heat like crazy. Nanna decided to throw a whole variety of ingredients into this pot and stirred them together. Why did she do this?

244. Like a bear

A bear does this in the winter. Many people will also do this after a heavy Thanksgiving meal. What will they do?

245. Thanksgiving holiday

Besides the bounty feast, there is another reason kids are excited about Thanksgiving time. Think long and hard about where you don't have to go. What is it?

246. Spice, naughty and nice

The pumpkin gets the credit for the pie, but I bring in that little bit of spice. What am I?

247. Stitched blanket

I am a thick and warm, like a blanket, but I have more layers. I am stitched up finely, and I will keep you warm on those cold fall nights. What am I?

248. Pie foundation

Inside of me can sit many ingredients. I am a solid foundation, both round and stable. I may feel hard, but I can be bitten into. As long as you have me, you can make pies of all types and sizes. What am I?

249. Feather side

There are two sides of every turkey. Which side has the feathers?

250. Dietary tofu entree

Turkeys love me because I am not made from them. I can be eaten as an entree for people with dietary restrictions. Those who do not eat living creatures will eat me. I am a strong source of protein known as tofu, and I am used to make a turkey substitute. What am I?

251. Dinner exceptions

You can eat almost anything for Thanksgiving dinner, but what are two things you absolutely cannot have?

252. Crazy pie

If a pumpkin pie and a pecan pie are standing on top of a ledge, which one will be crazy enough to jump off?

253. Twice or never

You will see me twice in November, but never on Thanksgiving. What am I?

254. An apple pie a day

One apple pie is dating another apple pie. He is concerned though because there seems to be a doctor that is smitten as well. The apple pie is going on a weeklong business trip and is worried about how to keep the doctor away. So, he gives his apple pie girlfriend seven apples. Why is that?

255. Broken oven pies

Jenny has two ovens that are broken. The top one can fit up to three pies, while the bottom one can fit up to four pies. How many pies will she be able to bake at the same time?

256. Baby vs adult eating contest

The baby turkey is much smaller than the adult stuffed turkey. If they have an eating contest, who would win?

257. Empty no more

Jamie has an empty stomach. How many cans of cranberry sauce can he eat so it's not empty anymore?

258. Buy and sell corn

If you buy 10 pieces of corn, sell five, and given another 10, eat six, given 10 more by your friend and eat five more, how many pieces of corn did you buy?

259. Different bedtime

Johnny goes to bed on the night before Thanksgiving. Tim goes to bed at the exact same moment and it is on Thanksgiving. How did this happen?

260. Turkey baseball

What is the most common call in a turkey baseball game?

261. Turkey plays basketball

Two turkeys are playing basketball. One turkey shoots the ball and misses. However, in doing so, he gets bumped aggressively by the other turkey. What does the first turkey do after this occurs?

262. Nearby corn

Why was the man able to know that there's corn nearby just by hearing it?

263. Turkey goes to White House

A turkey is headed to the White House for an event. On his way there, he is asked a question about the event that he did not fully hear. So, what does he say?

264. Safe bird on Thanksgiving

Even though the turkey is what people think of on Thanksgiving, I am actually the bird most likely to have been served on the First Thanksgiving. I like to float on the pond, looking calm, reminiscing about the days gone by. At least now, I can feel safe on Thanksgiving. What am I?

265. Turkeys for dinner

Brian buys three turkeys for Thanksgiving. James buys four turkeys for Thanksgiving. How many turkeys will Brian and James have for dinner?

266. Standing pairs

There are six people total standing in pairs on a field. The first two are Pilgrims. The next two are Native Americans. The next two are a Pilgrim and a Native American. Who will the next two pairs consist of?

267. Turkey for the band

Why was the turkey that was covered in various juices so valuable to the band?

268. Mary's bean varieties

Mary says she has ten different types of beans that she will cook for Thanksgiving. When observed by one of her guests, she notices that there are hundreds of beans on the counter. Was Mary lying?

269. Soda kept cold

Jenny goes out shopping on a cold and snowy Thanksgiving morning to buy some groceries. When she arrives home, she has no place in the fridge to put the sodas to keep them cold. When she looks outside, she gets her answer. What does she do?

270. Corn community party

Several members of the corn community are getting up on stage and throwing funny one-liners at other members of their community. What do you call corn that has succumbed to these one-liners?

271. When November ends

What should all turkeys decline at the end of November?

272. Corn festival

What is corns favorite festival?

273. Chicken no more

Why are turkeys served on Thanksgiving, rather than chickens?

274. Protect thyself

If a turkey had to protect itself, how would he do so?

275. Common denominator

What do turkeys and omelets have in common?

276. Run around the track

Tom the turkey is part of a track meet. He has never run on a track before. When the race starts, Tom gets completely confused and just starts running around in circles. How was he able to finish the race?

277. Long live ancient settlers

If the original settlers from the 1600s were still alive today, when it was a completely different world and culture, what would be the most surprising thing about them?

278. Walking west

A turkey wakes up in the morning and starts walking West. He leaves at 6 AM, and after walking one hour, the time is still 6 AM. Why is that?

279. Massive fire

There is a massive fire on a farm impacting many turkeys. Where would you bury the survivors?

280. Turkey lays egg

If a male turkey is standing on a rooftop right on the point, and it lays an egg, in what direction will the egg fall?

281. Turkey motorbike race

Two turkeys are racing, and both are on their motor bikes. One turkey is thinking of ways to make his bike faster, so he empties his gas tank. After doing so, his bike is 10 pounds lighter and able to go 10 miles per hour faster. In a 50-mile race, who will win?

282. Truck accident

If a truck carrying turkeys crashes on the highway and the lock doesn't break, how do you prevent the turkeys from running out?

283. Whose eggs are these

You have a turkey and a chicken in a barn. You come back after a week and notice a pile of eggs on one nest and about two eggs on the other. The turkey and chicken are not around. How do you know which nest belongs to what bird?

284. Food provision

What are two ways that Turkeys can provide food?

285. Turkey walks in a bank

If a turkey walks into a bank on Thanksgiving, what should it do?

286. Corn cob rows

When are the rows on a corn cob not straight?

287. Race to the cafeteria

Two turkeys walk into a school. One walks up to a locked door, right next to the cafeteria. The other one walks through a long hallway on the opposite side of the school. Who will reach the cafeteria first?

288. Turkey lost the band

What did the turkey lose to make it realize it could no longer be in a band?

289. Thanksgiving quiz

Whenever the teacher gives a pop quiz, about five out of her 20 students always get an A. When she gave a pop quiz on Thanksgiving Day related to the holiday, what percentage of the kids got an A grade?

290. Kernel count in a row

A fully eaten corn on the cob wants to count kernels in its rows. What row will he start with?

291. Covered by shell

I lay on the ground; I am covered from head to toe. It's difficult for me to come out of my shell. You will meet my mother on Thanksgiving. What am I?

292. Mark the calendar

When do you know that Halloween is officially over and Thanksgiving season is now upon us?

293. Evenly distributed leftovers

There is a total of 10 people around the dinner table. Michael wants to distribute nine leftover pieces of turkey evenly to all of his guests. He does so with no problems. How did he do it?

294. Solo dinner plan exposed

Mary is cooking in her kitchen by an open window. She does not want anyone to know that she is preparing Thanksgiving dinner because she plans to eat alone. She locks the doors and closes the living room curtains. She then goes back to cooking just as before. Her friends who walk by still know that she is cooking. What happened?

295. Failed sneaking plan

A family of turkeys is living in a house. The child turkey wants to go out, but the mother forbids. He goes up to his room and comes up with a plan. He will sneak out but will place pillows under the sheets to look like he is sleeping. After doing this, he sneaks out the window. Later in the night, his mother checks on him. She sees he is sleeping under the sheets, so she is about to leave, but then she notices her son's back peeking out of the sheets. At this point, she realizes it was not her son under the sheets. What gave it away first?

296. Brined at the same time

The chef was preparing two turkeys. The 12-pound turkey took four hours to brine, while the 10 pound one took three hours to brine. How long would it take if they brined them at the same time?

297. Turkey missed the party

Tom the turkey decides to sneak out of his third story window to go to a party. This is the only way he can get out. His friends are all waiting for him, but he never shows up. What happened to him?

298. Tofurkey meat

How much meat is in a tofurkey?

299. Corn in sugar

If corn drops into a sugar coating, what will happen?

300. Partners in crime

Why would a potato and corn be the perfect crime-fighting duo?

301. Secret kept secret

Why is corn the perfect thing to tell a secret to?

302. Raining turkeys

What do you call it when it starts raining turkeys?

Chapter 4: Easy Riddle Answers

1.
Answer: Stuffing

2.
Answer: Thanksgiving.

3.
Answer: Turkey

4.
Answer: Corn on the cob

5.
Answer: The dinner table.

6.
Answer: The oven.

7.
Answer: Something oven baked.

8.
Answer: Casserole.

9.
Answer: After Thanksgiving dinner.

10.
Answer: You won't need to. The can is still fully intact. Nothing spilled.

11.
Answer: Don't need to. I am already cooked.

12.
Answer: They are in a can, so already off the cob.

13.
Answer: Because corn does not grow on trees.

14.
Answer: Potato.

15.
Answer: Dessert.

16.
Answer: Wind.

17.
Answer: Pumpkin Pie.

18.
Answer: Drumstick.

19.
Answer: Family and Friends.

20.
Answer: When it's a corn belt.

21.
Answer: Gobble Gobble.

22.
Answer: The second turkey. It is moving slower but is already at the door and just needs to step outside.

23.
Answer: Silverware.

24.
Answer: Eight. Nobody has eaten them yet.

25.
Answer: Rolls.

26.
Answer: Football.

27.
Answer: Cranberry Sauce.

28.
Answer: Nothing. All of the food has been eaten.

29.
Answer: The cook.

30.
Answer: The turkey. It is still in the oven.

31.
Answer: Blue-berry.

32.
Answer: There was a second turkey that was brought out.

33.
Answer: Dinner time.

34.
Answer: The stuffing is inside of the turkey.

35.
Answer: Five turkeys. Two are just cooked.

36.
Answer: Glass.

37.
Answer: It's not meat; it's poultry.

38.
Answer: Parade.

39.
Answer: Pilgrim's pride.

40.
Answer: Ancestors.

41.
Answer: "I know what you feel like on the inside."

42.
Answer: They get the stuffing knocked out of them.

43.
Answer: Cornstalk.

44.
Answer: An egg.

45.
Answer: Wake up when the sun comes up and then go to bed when it's dark. He is staying up all during the day and only sleeping at night.

46.
Answer: Hot cocoa.

47.
Answer: Rake.

48.
Answer: None. Acorns don't grow on maple trees

49.
Answer: By buttering the skin.

50.
Answer: Corn by the bushels. I wonder how much one corn on the cob would be worth?

51.
Answer: Mashed potato.

52.
Answer: Thanksgiving turkey.

53.
Answer: Still three pieces.

54.
Answer: Late for dinner.

55.
Answer: Turkey.

56.
Answer: It will get eaten.

57.
Answer: Fowl play.

58.
Answer: Poul-tree.

59.
Answer: Dish.

60.
Answer: The one staying at the barn for obvious reasons.

61.
Answer: Buttercup

62.
Answer: Nothing. There's no meat, only bone.

63.
Answer: "May I get some bread, pudding?"

64.
Answer: Thanksgiving float.

65.
Answer: November.

66.
Answer: Aroma.

67.
Answer: Turkey roast.

68.
Answer: Turkey. The cornstalk is, well, too stalky.

69.
Answer: They gobble up the conversation.

70.
Answer: There is no fifth course.

71.
Answer: They are all guts and no brains.

72.
Answer: Indian corn.

73.
Answer: Bonfire.

74.
Answer: Domesticated turkeys don't fly.

75.
Answer: Feathers.

76.
Answer: Green beans.

77.
Answer: Apron.

78.
Answer: The son. There would be no class at the high school on Thanksgiving.

79.
Answer: Johnny. On a cold Thanksgiving Day, the lawn would not need to be mowed.

80.
Answer: His suitcase was too big.

81.
Answer: Two and a half minutes. Simple math.

82.
Answer: Only the ice cream needs to go in the freezer. The other things can go in the fridge.

83.
Answer: When his birthday fell on Thanksgiving, it was a leap year.

84.
Answer: Depends on how many stopovers the plane has. The only way a turkey can fly across the Atlantic.

85.
Answer: Corn Row.

86.
Answer: The turkey. It is actually going in the right direction.

87.
Answer: 20 days.

88.
Answer: Nowhere. They only put 10 chairs and have 10 guests. They forgot to put out two more for them.

89.
Answer: Table.

90.
Answer: There was more than one turkey.

91.
Answer: Turkey sandwich.

92.
Answer: Thunder

93.
Answer: The corn. It is full of kernels.

94.
Answer: White meat versus dark meat.

95.
Answer: They landed on Plymouth ROCK.

96.
Answer: Friday.

97.
Answer: His age.

98.
Answer: Pecan.

99.
Answer: One of the birds is not a turkey, but the other one is.

100.
Answer: Plymouth Rock.

101.
Answer: The snow is melted, so you won't have to clear it.

102.
Answer: He went to three different stores but did not buy something from all of the stores.

103.
Answer: One of the dinners was at his own house.

104.
Answer: 5 PM.

105.
Answer: Whoever's feathers matches his own feathers.

Chapter 5: Hard Riddle Answers

111.
Answer: Gravy.

107.
Answer: She started at 6 PM Thanksgiving night and finished at 6 AM in the morning the next day.

108.
Answer: Unfortunately, the turkey in question cannot be in two places at the same time. Phil would have to carve a different turkey.

109.
Answer: I-T.

110.
Answer: It does not matter, since they are trying to stay behind it.

111.
Answer: None. She still had five pieces.

112.
Answer: The ice cubes came from the contaminated water. They just did not have time to melt when the punch was first made.

113.
Answer: The match.

114.
Answer: Spread.

115.
Answer: You don't need to brine a turkey after cooking it.

116.
Answer: In the dictionary.

117.
Answer: A whole new world.

118.
Answer: The one that is missing feathers.

119.
Answer: T-H-A-T

120.
Answer: A cracked egg is already broken.

121.
Answer: None. The husk covers the corn but has no kernels of its own.

122.
Answer: The second one. The first one is still whole, so it has no slices.

123.
Answer: The skin is already removed since the potato is peeled.

124.
Answer: Just one actually. Corn is called maize in many parts of the world.

125.
Answer: Antarctica.

126.
Answer: Cinnamon.

127.
Answer: The turkey's name is Thursday.

128.
Answer: Neither one. The library will be closed on Thanksgiving.

129.
Answer: Cornbread.

130.
Answer: The Mayflower.

131.
Answer: Pilgrims.

132.
Answer: Pecan Pie.

133.
Answer: Yam.

134.
Answer: Still one wishbone. It's just in two pieces.

135.
Answer: Thanksgiving is on the fourth Thursday of the month.

136.
Answer: If the turkey is going in the same direction, it won't cross the same road again.

137.
Answer: A marshmallow

138.
Answer: No time since the ship is already built.

139.
Answer: Dressing.

140.
Answer: Ham.

141.
Answer: Giblets.

142.
Answer: Since they are partners, they both won gold.

143.
Answer: A feather duster.

144.
Answer: None. The glass is empty.

145.
Answer: They began at 11:55 PM and finished at 12:05 AM.

146.
Answer: They were already at the same spot since they began running from the same point. And since they are running in opposite directions from the same point, they will likely never reach the same spot again.

147.
Answer: Because he was grateful for what he had.

148.
Answer: The turkey, of course.

149.
Answer: It was walking on the overpass above the road where the traffic was.

150.
Answer: Cornucopia.

151.
Answer: The letter T.

152.
Answer: It was not dressed.

153.
Answer: Because they were stuffed.

154.
Answer: A wild turkey.

155.
Answer: The one on the East end because it actually goes inside the store, while the other runs INTO the store. Ouch!

156.
Answer: Everyone was making dinner requests.

157.
Answer: Tom Turkey. He just lost his hat. His name did not change.

158.
Answer: There will be no third house. You already visited both grandparents.

159.
Answer: A-corn.

160.
Answer: Ornithology (bird science).

161.
Answer: Ninth row.

162.
Answer: At the butterball.

163.
Answer: No time. It is ready made and already cooked.

164.
Answer: The first Thanksgiving.

165.
Answer: It was a dark meat.

166.
Answer: Bone Voyage.

167.
Answer: Four-fathers.

168.
Answer: Because turkeys gobble.

169.
Answer: There are still 10. He collected the five leaves from the tree and not the ground.

170.
Answer: Apple Pie.

171.
Answer: Corn casserole.

172.
Answer: He began eating it right before midnight on the last day of November and finished it shortly after midnight on December first.

173.
Answer: Not everyone sat at the dinner table.

174.
Answer: He spends 60 minutes at the first two houses, and 30 minutes at the last house.

175.
Answer: Squash.

176.
Answer: He won't. They are both going to their friend's house, but not the same friend.

177.
Answer: Native Americans.

178.
Answer: Leaves.

179.
Answer: Orchard.

180.
Answer: Stew.

181.
Answer: Pilgrim's hat.

182.
Answer: A table.

183.
Answer: The two bowls are already split evenly.

184.
Answer: They make a club sandwich.

185.
Answer: Roosters don't lay eggs.

186.
Answer: They have feathers.

187.
Answer: No time. The turkeys are already carved.

188.
Answer: United States of America.

189.
Answer: Their feet.

190.
Answer: Any day. It's just eaten more commonly on Thanksgiving.

191.
Answer: One. Once you use it on one, the can is not technically full anymore.

192.
Answer: A total of 20 guests were there, but not all of them arrived at the same time.

193.
Answer: Just take away the S.

194.
Answer: He won't need containers since the gravy is eaten right away.

195.
Answer: Still a turkey.

196.
Answer: Turkey float.

197.
Answer: Brine.

198.
Answer: Pilgrimage.

199.
Answer: The three people are a grandmother, her daughter and granddaughter. The grandmother is also a mother, her daughter is also a mother.

200.
Answer: Since the pie is cooked, it won't take any.

201.
Answer: The first two people just took the bowl but did not take anything out of it.

202.
Answer: Depends on who cooked it. If both groups cooked a turkey, there would be two different turkeys.

203.
Answer: With their hands.

204.
Answer: Jimmy is also a turkey. James was seeing Jimmy as well as the other turkey.

205.
Answer: Seven is the name of the person who buys a turkey.

206.
Answer: Of course. That's why there are so many leftovers.

207.
Answer: Three.

208.
Answer: The food court.

209.
Answer: Those two hands were on the clock.

210.
Answer: 10. None of them have been eaten yet.

211.
Answer: Per the instructions, only half a packet of brine was needed for each turkey.

Chapter 6: Difficult Riddle Answers

214.
Answer: Suzy. The bank will be closed.

213.
Answer: The neighbor to the right. There was no way for him to know that he was at work when nobody knows when the turkey was stolen.

214.
Answer: The person with the corn. They probably have not had time to hide it yet.

215.
Answer: The farmer has the turkeys now, but not all of them were born on the same farm.

216.
Answer: Food coma.

217.
Answer: Centerpiece.

218.
Answer: Nap.

219.
Answer: A Tradition.

220.
Answer: There will be no school bus the day after Thanksgiving since there will be no school.

221.
Answer: Inside an Orchard.

222.
Answer: Voyage.

223.
Answer: Wishbone.

224.
Answer: First, go to the one that's 8 miles away, then the one that's 15 miles away and then the one that's 10 miles away on the other side. This will allow the shortest driving distances.

225.
Answer: Tablecloth.

226.
Answer: Leftovers.

227.
Answer: Drumsticks.

228.
Answer: They would not be able to sail in the same direction. They have already reached land.

229.
Answer: On their feet.

230.
Answer: Pilgrims, Of course.

231.
Answer: None. Pecans don't grow on maple trees.

232.
Answer: The turkey. The pumpkin has no legs.

233.
Answer: No time. You won't carve the drumstick but will just eat it whole.

234.
Answer: James loves the white meat; Tom loves the dark meat, and Michael loves the instruments.

235.
Answer: Tom. The library will be closed.

236.
Answer: The turkey is also dressed up.

237.
Answer: Seeing his friend on the center of a table.

238.
Answer: None. The pumpkin is carved out and has nothing left inside.

239.
Answer: Neither. They crossed it at the same time.

240.
Answer: Neither one. The food was all eaten by everyone else while they were competing with each other.

241.
Answer: Harvest moon.

242.
Answer: A hey stack.

243.
Answer: Because it is a melting pot.

244.
Answer: Hibernate.

245.
Answer: Long weekend.

246.
Answer: Pumpkin spice.

247.
Answer: Quilt.

248.
Answer: Pie crust.

249.
Answer: The outside.

250.
Answer: Tofurkey.

251.
Answer: Breakfast and lunch.

252.
Answer: Pecan pie, because they are all nuts.

253.
Answer: The letter "E".

254.
Answer: An apple a day keeps the doctor away. Seven will keep him away for a whole week.

255.
Answer: None, both of the ovens are broken.

256.
Answer: The baby turkey, because the adult turkey is already stuffed.

257.
Answer: One. After that, his stomach won't be empty anymore.

258.
Answer: 10. The other pieces were either given to you, sold or eaten.

259.
Answer: Johnny and Tim live in different time zones.

260.
Answer: Fowl ball.

261.
Answer: Calls Fowl.

262.
Answer: He had the ear of corn.

263.
Answer: Pardon.

264.
Answer: Duck.

265.
Answer: Brian will have three. James will have four. We never said they would be at the same dinner.

266.
Answer: Nothing. There are only six people total.

267.
Answer: Because it had a strong baste. It's all about that baste.

268.
Answer: No, she just said she has 10 different kinds of beans, not how many beans she has altogether.

269.
Answer: She puts the drinks outside since it is cold and snowy.

270.
Answer: Roasted corn.

271.
Answer: Dinner reservations.

272.
Answer: Corn-ival.

273.
Answer: They are easier to gobble up.

274.
Answer: He would grab his turkey club.

275.
Answer: They both come from an egg.

276.
Answer: Easily, he just ran around in circles, which is what a track is.

277.
Answer: It would be their age.

278.
Answer: He was walking West, so he crosses a time zone that was one hour behind his starting point.

279.
Answer: Nowhere. You don't bury survivors.

280.
Answer: Male turkeys don't lay eggs.

281.
Answer: The turkey with the full gas tank as the other turkey's bike will not make it to the end without gas.

282.
Answer: The turkeys are safe. The lock did not break.

283.
Answer: Turkeys usually lay much fewer eggs than chickens.

284.
Answer: Through their meat and through their eggs.

285.
Answer: Turn and walk back out. The bank is closed..

286.
Answer: When the corn is cut up.

287.
Answer: The one walking through the long hallway as the other one won't be able to open the locked door.

288.
Answer: It lost its drumsticks.

289.
Answer: None. There is no school on thanksgiving, hence, no test.

290.
Answer: The kernels are all gone. It was fully eaten.

291.
Answer: Turkey egg.

292.
Answer: November 1st.

293.
Answer: There are 10 people total including Michael. There are only nine guests, so he was able to distribute the nine pieces of turkey evenly. He did not take one.

294.
Answer: She was still cooking by her open window in the kitchen.

295.
Answer: She didn't see any feathers.

296.
Answer: The same amount of time. They are just being brined at the same time, but still will take the same number of hours.

297.
Answer: He was stuck on the windowsill. He had no way of getting down because he can't fly.

298.

Answer: None, it has tofu.

299.

Answer: You will have candy corn.

300.

Answer: They can be each other's eye and ears. The eyes of a potato, the ear of corn.

301.

Answer: They have ears to listen, but no mouth to talk. And no eyes to see who is telling them the secret. A perfect listening ear.

302.

Answer: Fowl weather.

One Final Thing...

Thank for making it through to the end of *Fun Halloween Riddles and Trick Questions for Kids and Family*, let's hope it was fun, challenging and able to provide you and your family with all of the entertainment you needed for this rainy day (or sunny afternoon)!

Did You Enjoy the Book?

If you did, please let us know by leaving a review on AMAZON. Review let Amazon know that we are creating quality material for children. Even a few words and ratings would go a long way. We would like to thank you in advance for your time.

If you have any comments, or suggestions for improvement for other books, we would love to hear from and you and can contact us at riddleland@riddlelandforkids.com

Your comments are greatly valued, and the book have already been revised and improved as a result of helpful suggestions from readers.

Other Fun Children Books for The Kids!
Riddles Series

Encourage your kids to think outside of the box with these Fun and Creative Riddles!

Get them on Amazon

Try Not to Laugh Challenge Series

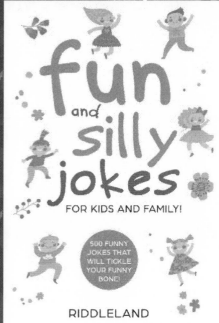

Would you rather series

Get them on Amazon
or our website at www.riddlelandforkids.com

Get the Bonus Book!

https://bit.ly/riddlelandbonusbook

Thank you for buying this book, We would like to share a special bonus as a token of appreciation. It is collection 50 original jokes, riddles and 2 funny stories

About the Author

Riddleland is a mom + dad run publishing company. We are passionate about creating fun and innovative books to help children develop their reading skill and fall in love with reading. If you have suggestions for us or want to work with us, shoot us an email at riddleland@riddlelandforkids.com

Check out our website to see what exciting book we are working on next!
www.riddlelandforkids.com

Our favorite family quote

"Creativity is area in which younger people have a tremendous advantage since they have an endearing habit of always questioning past wisdom and authority." – Bill Hewlett

Made in the USA
Middletown, DE
14 November 2019